The Usborne
Unworry Book

Written by Alice James

Designed and illustrated by Stephen Moncrieff

Additional illustration by
Cristina Martin Recasens
and Freya Harrison

Expert advice from
Dr. Angharad Rudkin,
clinical psychologist,
University of Southampton

WE ALL WORRY

Worries are annoying, but they're also normal, and unfortunately pretty common. EVERYONE worries at some point, and some of us worry a lot.

Worrying isn't a bad thing, and often it can help you do a good job or be a better person. But it's important to be able to cope with worries so they don't stop you from living your life.

This book helps make sense of worries and is full of ideas to calm you down and distract you, as well as places to get your worries out.

UNWORRY TOOLKIT

Emergency calm-down techniques for panicky moments, on pages 54-55.

Breathing exercises to relax and unwind, on page 23.

Diary entries to figure out your feelings, on page 57.

Worry monsters you can imagine and tell to GO AWAY, on page 16.

An unworry island to design and escape to whenever you need it, on pages 20-21.

And much more...

WHY DO WE WORRY?

Worries exist to help you manage risk and stay safe – like an ALARM SYSTEM that goes off when you're in danger. When you worry, chemicals are released in your body, so you're ready to react to danger:

YOUR BODY TEMPERATURE INCREASES

YOUR HEART PUMPS FASTER

YOUR HANDS GET SWEATY AND SHAKY

In extreme circumstances worrying can save your life – for example by stopping you from running out in front of a car. But you don't need it to survive day-to-day. Most of the time when you worry, it's just your alarm system over-reacting. Some people's alarms go off more than others. The important thing is not how much you worry, but how you deal with it...

...AND THAT'S WHERE THIS BOOK COMES IN.

HOW THIS BOOK WILL HELP

This book will try to help you deal with worries, from little random ones to BIG overwhelming ones. It might not make them go away COMPLETELY, but here are three ways it might help a little.

1. BY HELPING YOU FIGURE OUT THE PROBLEM

It can be useful just to work out HOW you feel - are you worried, or is the feeling actually excitement or nerves? Being able to recognize how you feel is called EMOTIONAL AWARENESS, and you can find out about it on these pages:

There's a **map of emotions** to wander through on pages **8-9**.

Find out how to use **colors** rather than words to **express your feelings** on pages **26-27**.

There is also information about the **science** of worry and emotions, on pages **22, 44, 64 & 88**.

4

2. BY GIVING YOU A PLACE TO WORRY

Sometimes when you worry it can just build up and up, with nowhere to go. There are lots of places in this book where you can get worries out of your head and onto paper:

Divide your worries into ones you can and can't **control**, on pages **36-37**.

Fill in a **diary** for a few days, on pages **56-61**.

Break **big worries** down into **little chunks**, on pages **80-81**.

Write, draw or doodle anything **on your mind** on pages **76-77**.

If worries are **stopping you from sleeping**, get them out of your head on pages **90-91**.

Put your worries on a **worry shelf** on pages **92-93**.

3. BY DISTRACTING YOU

You don't always need to focus on the worry itself to feel better. It's often best just to think about something completely different - while your brain is occupied with other things, the worries get pushed out.

You might also find that while you're distracted, the worry disappears entirely, sorting itself out quietly in the back of your mind.

This book is full of stuff to distract you.

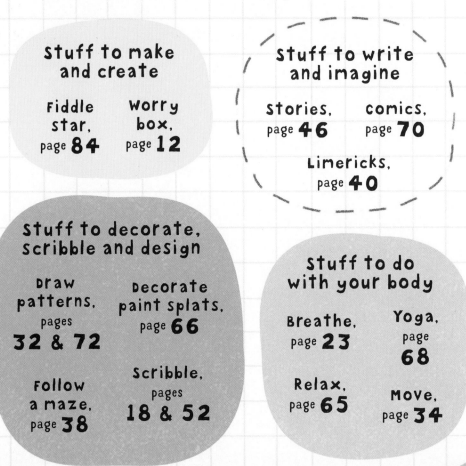

Stuff to make and create

Fiddle star, page **84**

Worry box, page **12**

Stuff to write and imagine

Stories, page **46**

Comics, page **70**

Limericks, page **40**

Stuff to decorate, scribble and design

Draw patterns, pages **32 & 72**

Decorate paint splats, page **66**

Follow a maze, page **38**

Scribble, pages **18 & 52**

Stuff to do with your body

Breathe, page **23**

Yoga, page **68**

Relax, page **65**

Move, page **34**

You might feel a little awkward trying some of these things. It doesn't always come naturally to think about emotions, and doodling or designing worry monsters might feel a little silly at first. But that's normal too, and OK. Just give it a try and see how it works for you.

Everything in the book has been checked and recommended by a psychologist – a brain and behavior expert. Everything in here is designed to be helpful – there's a range of stuff to help all sorts of different people, so there should be something in here that helps YOU.

USBORNE QUICKLINKS

For advice, support, and more unworry activities, go to www.usborne.com/quicklinks and type in the keyword UNWORRY. Please follow the online safety guidelines at the Usborne Quicklinks website.

HOW DO YOU FEEL?

Sometimes it's really helpful just to try putting your finger on exactly how you're feeling.

If you're struggling to name a feeling, take a wander through this EMOTIONS MAP. You can come back to this page again and again. Add words to the map if what you feel isn't here.

UPSET

EXCITED

HOPEFUL

HAPPY

IRRITABLE

ANNOYED

FRIGHTENED

RELAXED

You might feel one, or two, or twenty emotions.

SCARED

TIRED

CHEERFUL

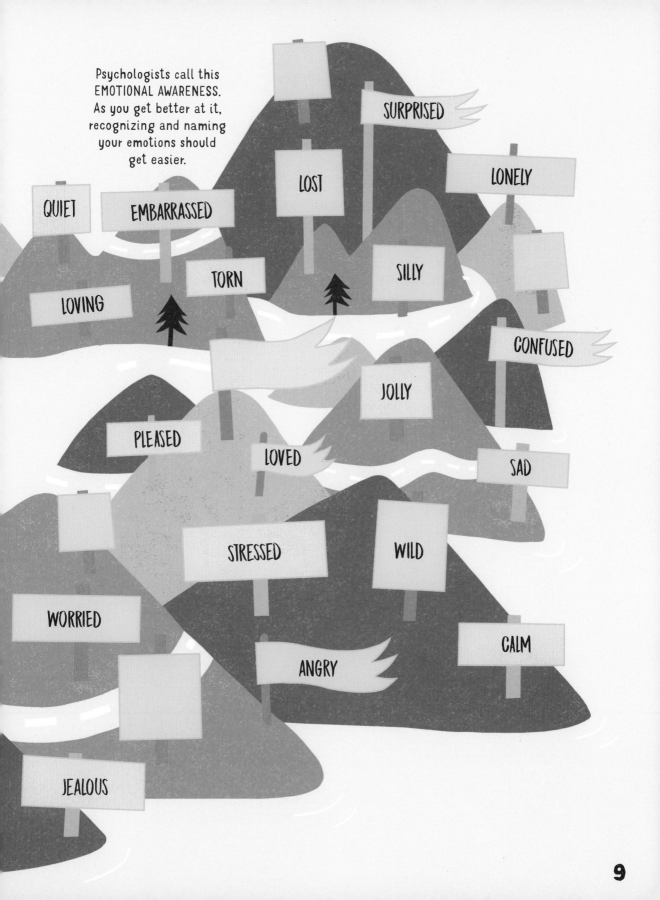

Psychologists call this EMOTIONAL AWARENESS. As you get better at it, recognizing and naming your emotions should get easier.

PEACEFUL PENCILS

Psychologists often recommend a technique called MINDFULNESS for anyone who might be worrying.

Mindfulness is all about focusing on small details in the here and now. Color in this pattern, and as you do, only think about the things you can feel, hear and smell, right now. Go slowly, and deliberately, and take time to wrap yourself up in it.

Listen to the sound the pen or pencil makes as it brushes across the paper.

Notice the glistening wet ink of your pen, or the grain of the paper as your pencil draws across it.

Smell the pages of the book.

Feel the ridges of your pencil, or the plastic barrel of your pen.

Smell the wood of your pencil, or the ink of your pen.

Feel the textures of this page under your fingers. Does it feel warm, or cool?

WORRY BOX

Writing down a worry helps to get it OUT OF YOUR HEAD. Try making a worry box to get rid of worries you're jotting down. Turn the box into a creature, and imagine it EATING up the worries.

YOU WILL NEED:

AN EMPTY ENVELOPE, JAR, TISSUE BOX OR TUB PENS, DECORATIONS, GLUE

It can be made of anything you can put stuff in.

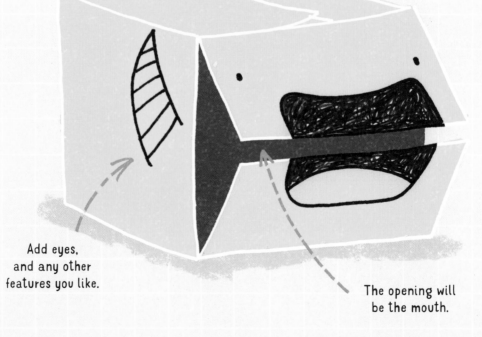

Add eyes, and any other features you like.

The opening will be the mouth.

Then start decorating.
Here are some ideas, but you
can use anything you find.

STRING HAIR

PIPE CLEANER GLASSES

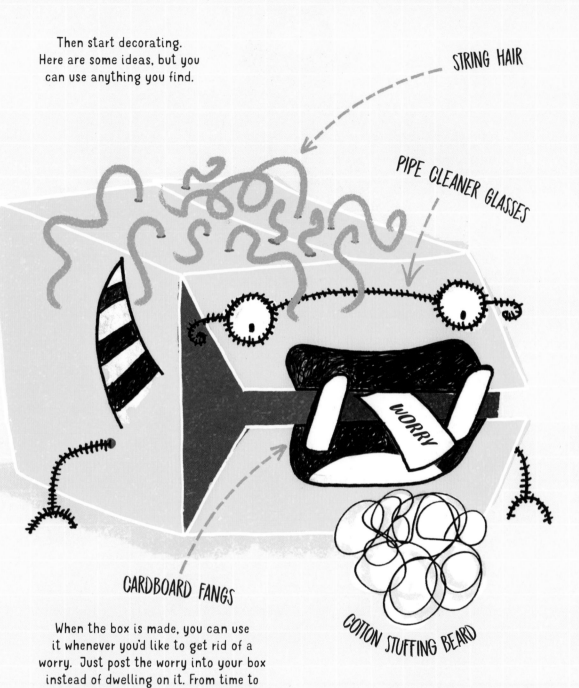

WORRY

CARDBOARD FANGS

COTTON STUFFING BEARD

When the box is made, you can use
it whenever you'd like to get rid of a
worry. Just post the worry into your box
instead of dwelling on it. From time to
time, empty the box out into a recycling
bin, so the worries don't build up.

WORRY

Alternatively, you could just
SCRUNCH them up and THROW them
away. Sometimes worries just need
to be chucked away entirely.

13

WHAT IFS

"WHAT IF I'M LATE?"

"WHAT IF IT GOES WRONG?"

"WHAT IF I CAN'T DO IT?"

A LOT OF OUR WORRIES START WITH THE WORDS "WHAT IF..."

This is really normal. Our brains often jump to the WORST CASE SCENARIO - the worst possible thing you can think of happening.

Many worries are actually really simple to solve, but once you start to worry you get more and more anxious, and find it hard to see rational, sensible solutions.

"WHAT IF I FORGET TO BRING PENCILS TO A TEST?"

COULD BE SOLVED BY

Asking someone for a spare! You could ask a friend, a teacher, or borrow one from a classroom.

Some "what if" worries can be a little harder, because they are more emotional. That doesn't mean they don't have answers though.

"WHAT IF I HAVE AN ARGUMENT WITH MY FRIEND?"

COULD BE SOLVED BY

Talking it through, apologizing if you need to, and working it out together. The falling out doesn't need to be permanent.

Making a new friend. People change over time, and friendships change with them.

It might not work for every worry, but thinking of some logical, simple answers to your "what if" questions can be a really effective way of calming down. Try it for yourself, and see if it works. There's an activity to help you with "what if" worries on the next page.

It can be really helpful to think about your worries as a character, completely separate from yourself. Psychologists call this unworry technique EXTERNALIZING.

Use the space below to design a "what if" creature. Whenever a worry pops into your head, just imagine the creature and tell it to go away, or turn its volume down – DIMINISH it, LOSE it, get RID of it...

You might find your creature looks silly, or ridiculous. That's actually really useful. It's good to remember your worries are just thoughts. You can beat them, and even laugh at them.

It can also help to create an ANTI-what-if creature - a wise, reasonable, logical character that can help you think of those simple solutions. Design yours here.

IT COULD BE A:

WIZARD   ANGEL   WISE OWL

It might feel silly to draw a worry gremlin, or
anti-worry wizard, but psychologists think it's really helpful to
externalize worries. If you don't want to draw them, you could
describe them in words instead, or just draw a blob.

SCRIBBLE

Rather than shouting,
crying or getting angry when you're worried,
try SCRIBBLING the anxiety away. Scratch,
scrawl and scribble on this page until the
worry subsides and you feel calmer.

Whenever you feel worried,
you could get a piece of paper
out of the recycling bin and
scribble all over it. Then scrunch
it up and throw it away again.

UNWORRY ISLAND

Design your own UNWORRY ISLAND, a place you can imagine and visit whenever you need to, especially at bedtime if worries are stopping you from sleeping.

What's the weather like?

Where do you stay?
A hut? A treehouse?
An igloo?

Who else is there with you? Or are you by yourself?

What do you eat? Fruit from the trees? Fish from the sea? An endless supply of ice cream from a cafe?

It doesn't have to be realistic. This is YOUR unworry island - it can be absolutely anything you want, as long as there are no worries there.

The more you use your island to relax, the more helpful it'll be. Scientists call this process CONDITIONING. You train your body to RELAX whenever you imagine the island. So don't just visit the island once, pop back again and again, and add or change things whenever you like.

THE SCIENCE OF STRESS

Worrying causes a lot of physical changes in your body. When you get stressed, your body releases chemicals called HORMONES.

The most famous worry hormone is ADRENALINE. Adrenaline gets your body ready for what scientists call...

the
FIGHT OR FLIGHT
response.

In prehistoric times adrenaline prepared people to FIGHT dangerous animals, or FLEE from them, in order to save their lives. This is how it works...

Making your heart beat faster. This gets more blood flowing around your body to deliver vital stuff your muscles need to GO.

Making you breathe in short shallow gasps. It's trying to get more oxygen into your blood quickly, to FUEL the running or fighting.

Making you very ALERT, AWARE and ON EDGE, so you can respond really fast.

After a few minutes, or sometimes hours, adrenaline GOES AWAY – levels of the hormone go back down, and you feel normal again.

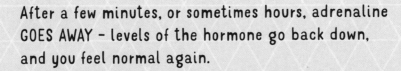

AND BREATHE...

Once you know what worry does to your body, it's easier to make yourself feel better.

Adrenaline makes you want to breathe in QUICKLY. This makes you more and more stressed, as if you're running out of air.

Keep both feet on the floor, shoulder-width apart. This is called GROUNDING, and it makes you feel instantly more calm, reassured and in control.

Breathe in through your nose for **3** seconds, **ALL THE WAY INTO YOUR CHEST.** Breathe out for **3** seconds through your mouth.

Keep going until your breathing feels steady, your heart slows down, and you feel relaxed.

LAUGH!

Scientists have found that when your muscles move and tense as you LAUGH, chemicals called ENDORPHINS are released in your brain. Endorphins make you feel happier and relaxed, and also reduce the amount of stress chemicals in your body. So chuckle, giggle, chortle or guffaw, and see if it helps your worries go away...

In this box write down or draw things that you find really funny.

Silly words

Animals doing human things

Think about the last time
you laughed so much it
hurt. What was it about?

Use this space to write down any jokes
you like – or you could make up your own.

SCRIBBLE YOUR FEELINGS

You don't have to write or talk about your worries to figure them out. Just try doodling in a way that reflects your mood, so you can see what your mood LOOKS LIKE. So, grab some colors and start SCRIBBLING.

If you're feeling quiet, or sad, you could use gentle, small movements with the pencil.

If you're feeling angry you might press hard, or if you're feeling anxious you might scribble and scrawl.

Many shades are traditionally associated with certain feelings.

RED ANGRY ADVENTUROUS

ORANGE FIERY WARM EXCITED

YELLOW HAPPY CHEERFUL OPTIMISTIC

GREEN JEALOUS EMBARRASSED PEACEFUL

BLUE CALM SAD THOUGHTFUL

PURPLE POWERFUL MAGIC CONFIDENT

BLACK MOODY SCARED MYSTERIOUS

GRAY SAD GRUMPY QUIET

You could use these ideas, or make up your own.

You could use one color for one emotion, or a range to represent a scramble of feelings.

RIP IT!

Find some paper, and tear it up into as many tiny pieces as you can. Stick them all over this page, and create a snowstorm of ripped paper.

When the page is full,
count the pieces. How
many are there?

Your brain isn't very good at
doing more than one thing at
once. If it's focusing on this, it's
NOT focusing on worries.

BUILD YOURSELF UP

Sometimes you might have worries that aren't about stuff going on around you, but about you yourself - "Can I do it?", "Am I good enough?", "I feel as if I failed."

You can FIGHT these worries by telling yourself GOOD things LOUDER than your brain tells you bad things. This is known as POSITIVE SELF TALK in the psychology world. Fill this page with positive things about yourself, and reminders that you're doing a good job.

Things you're good at.

Things you're working on or improving at.

Things you like about yourself.

I look good in my new hat.

If you're struggling, think about things your friends think you're good at, or like about you. The things you write might feel cheesy, but BUILDING YOURSELF UP can help banish worries. Come back to this page for a boost of confidence whenever you feel you need one.

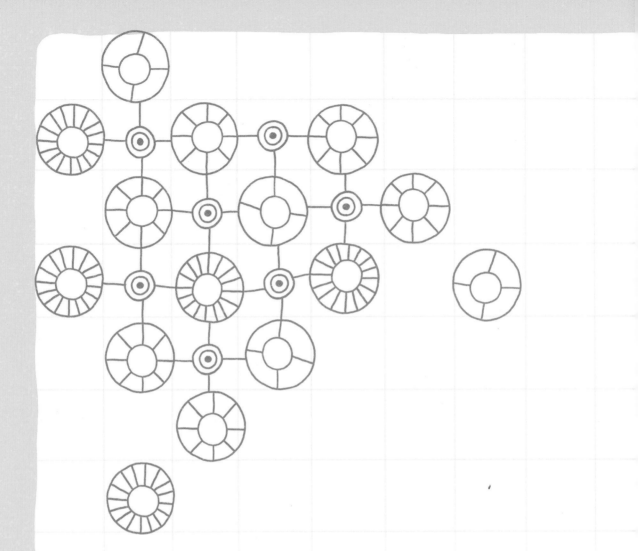

Sometimes, when you distract yourself
with something, you'll find that whatever
you were worrying about has just stopped
feeling like a problem without you noticing.

PATTERNS

Here's some more peaceful, focused
distraction. Continue these patterns
across the page, concentrating on the
shapes you're making and using all the
space. You could color them in too.

MOVE IT, MOVE IT!

Being active releases chemicals called ENDORPHINS in your brain. Endorphins are feel-good chemicals that give you a big BOOST.

Here are some ideas for getting active that are quick and easy to do at home, or out and about. They may sound obvious and even a bit silly, but don't worry – just GO FOR IT.

DANCE

Put some music on and DANCE for a few minutes.

Make your dance as...

BIG SMALL FUNKY or WILD

...as you like.

Just move!

JUMP

Big
jumps

Hop jumps

Jumping jacks

Long jumps

STEP

Find some stairs and walk up
and down them a few times, until
you're out of breath.

UP

UP

UP

DOWN

DOWN

Phew!

Scientists have
shown that being
PHYSICALLY active can improve
your MENTAL wellbeing. It can
also improve your SELF-ESTEEM and
give you a sense of ACHIEVEMENT, and
provide a great DISTRACTION.

More moving = less worrying,
so get to it!

UNDER CONTROL

Some worries and problems are within your control, and have simple solutions you can find right away. But there are a lot of worries that are totally OUT of your control.

Learning the difference between those worries is really important. Think about the things you worry about. Write any you CAN control on this page, and any you CAN'T control on the opposite page.

THINGS YOU CAN CONTROL

Things you say

36

THINGS YOU CAN'T CONTROL

Stuff on
the news

The weather

Things on this page might still be really worrying. But the fact
you can't change them means there's no point spending lots of
time thinking about them. Learning to LET GO of these things
is one of the greatest unworry techniques there is.

MAZE

Find your way through this maze to the finish.
Focus on keeping your pencil between the lines.
Think of it as finding your way through a tangle
of worries, and out the other side.

START

FINISH

LIMERICKS

Keep your brain busy and make yourself chuckle by writing some humorous poems called LIMERICKS. Limericks work like this:

The first, second and fifth lines rhyme, and each of these lines has 8 or 9 syllables.

1 An elderly fellow called Keith
2 Had mislaid his set of false teeth.
3 They'd been left on a chair,
4 He forgot they were there,
5 Sat down - and was bitten beneath.

The third and fourth lines are shorter, and have their own rhyme.

Each of these lines has 5 or 6 syllables.

Limericks are often nonsensical and funny.

Try finishing off these limericks. Use a pencil so you can change it if you want to.

There was a young man made of tin,

- -

- -

- -

- -

There once was an alien called Zars,

An old penguin was skating on ice,

Try a whole limerick
with your own first line:

CALM

Calm. Four letters, one little word, but a big, wonderful feeling.

Write it out really small

Now really

BIG

In your swirliest, fanciest writing

Upside down

Backwards

Press as lightly as you can

Try writing it with the hand you don't normally use

Write it in a
Thick
chunky
outline

Fill the letters in soothing shapes

THE SCIENCE OF BEING NEGATIVE

Annoyingly, humans are built to notice and focus on NEGATIVES more than POSITIVES. Negative things like dangers, illnesses and bad weather could affect the survival of prehistoric people, so it was important to spot them and think about them. But our brains still do this today.

Scientists have a fancy term for this:

NEGATIVITY BIAS

When something bad happens, your brain BUZZES with more ELECTRICITY than it does for good stuff.

That means you are hard-wired to process negative things. This is one of the reasons people worry so much.

ON THE POSITIVE

The good news is you can do something about your brain's built-in negativity bias by thinking really hard about POSITIVE THINGS.

Think about things you're REALLY LOOKING FORWARD TO and write them here.

It could be a trip, lunch, a TV show, seeing a friend - anything you're EXCITED about.

ONCE UPON A TIME...

Try to forget about any worries by taking your mind somewhere completely different. This is sometimes called ESCAPISM. It might not solve the problem, but it can help you feel better for a while.

Use this story starter, and keep it going – immerse yourself in your story, in a land far, far away.

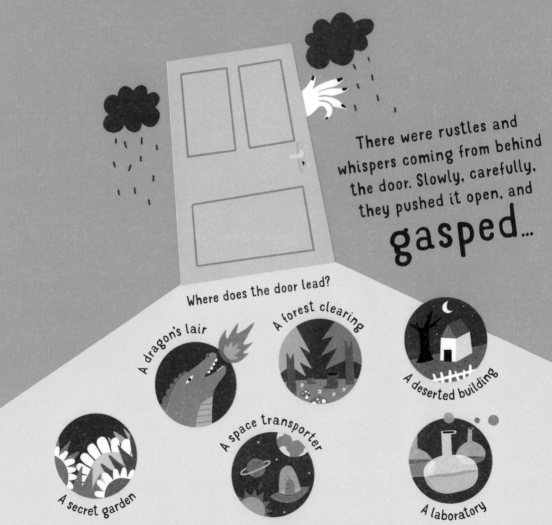

There were rustles and whispers coming from behind the door. Slowly, carefully, they pushed it open, and

gasped...

Where does the door lead?

A dragon's lair

A forest clearing

A deserted building

A secret garden

A space transporter

A laboratory

MOOD GRID

Pick colors for each of the moods below. Then color in
the first box in the grid on the right, depending on
how you're feeling. Come back to this page once a day,
filling in one more box each time.

This is about looking inside and seeing how you are -
recognizing emotions, and LETTING YOURSELF feel them.

You could use the shades suggested on page 27, or
choose the colors these emotions feel like to YOU.

Happy   Sad   Worried   Tired   Excited   Not sure

If some of these aren't emotions you feel very much,
cross them out and write new ones. For example you
might change "sad" to "confused" or "grumpy."

Most days you'll probably feel more than one thing,
but color in the mood you feel the MOST that day.

If you use "not sure" a lot, take a look at the emotions map
on page 8-9 to see if any of those words help you
put your finger on what you feel.

TAKE A LINE FOR A WALK

Take a few minutes to distract your brain from any worrisome wanders that it might be going on. Follow this line, and continue it ALL OVER the page. Try to make sure the pencil doesn't leave the paper.

You could draw something in particular, or just let the pencil walk randomly over the page in a scribble or swirl.

IF YOU'RE IN A PANIC...

Sometimes, when worries build up a lot, you can start to panic. Your heart beats quickly, you feel breathless and shaky, and you get a heavy feeling in your chest. If this happens, try this, the MINDFULNESS 5.

NOTICE **5** things you can see

LISTEN TO **4** things you can hear

FEEL **3** things you can touch

FIND **2** things you can smell

IS THERE **1** thing you can taste?

Try it wherever you are now to see how it works. Focus on your senses to find a mindfulness 5, and write them here.

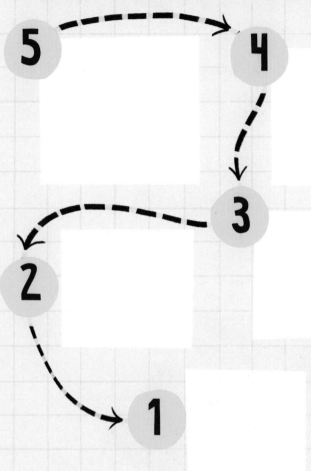

This is a useful tool to remember in really panicky moments. It will help to ground you, and reduce your anxiety. By the time you've found the things, you might even have forgotten what you were worrying about.

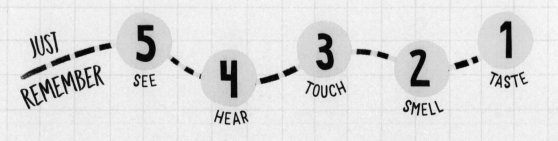

JUST REMEMBER

5 SEE

4 HEAR

3 TOUCH

2 SMELL

1 TASTE

FIVE-DAY DIARY

Jotting down what's going on in your life, and how you feel about it, can help you work out what you tend to worry about. It can also improve your EMOTIONAL AWARENESS - being able to identify your feelings.

Over the next five days, try filling in all the boxes on the next few pages. If you find it helpful, or enjoyable, you could use the simple layout to start keeping your own journal in a separate notebook.

DAY 1

In here you could draw a face of how you felt, or add a number from 1-10.

Date

Day

Weather

Overall mood

What happened today

Good stuff

Not-so-good stuff

Any worries on your mind

DAY 2

Date

Day

Weather

Overall mood

What happened today

Good stuff

Not-so-good stuff

Any worries on your mind

DAY 3

Date

Day

Weather

Overall mood

What happened today

Good stuff

Not-so-good stuff

Any worries on your mind

DAY 4

Date

Day

Weather

Overall mood

What happened today

Good stuff

Not-so-good stuff

Any worries on your mind

DAY 5

Date

Day

Weather

Overall mood

What happened today

Good stuff

Not-so-good stuff

Any worries on your mind

WHAT'S IMPORTANT?

Psychologists think you worry less if you focus on the stuff you VALUE in life, more than your aims or goals. You can't fail at a value, or get it wrong, and thinking about what's important to you can help you make decisions and work out who you are.

HERE'S A LIST OF VALUES. WHICH ONES MATTER MOST TO YOU?

Kindness
Be helpful and compassionate towards everyone

Power
Influence people and be in charge

Cooperation
Work well with others, and bring people together

Independence
Support yourself, and find your own way

comedy
Find the funny side, and make others laugh

Adventure
Explore, find, and experience new things

Honesty
Be truthful and open with yourself and others

Trust
Be loyal and reliable

Justice
Be fair, and aware of what is right and wrong

Equality
Treat everyone as equals, whoever they are

skills
Improve and develop your talents and abilities

courage
Be brave, fight negative things, and keep going

Spirituality
Feel connected to big ideas and beliefs

Creativity
Invent, design and make

Hard work
Be dedicated and committed

challenge
Make yourself do new or difficult things

curiosity
Discover, ask questions, explore and learn

If what you value most isn't here, write it in this box:

Choose the SIX of these values that are the MOST important to you, and write them here:

1. _____

2. _____

3. _____

4. _____

5. _____

6. _____

THE SCIENCE OF FEAR

Sometimes you worry even if there's no real reason to.

This pesky feeling of fear comes from a place in the brain called the

AMYGDALA.

The amygdala's response is AUTOMATIC – you have absolutely no control over it. That's why, even when REALLY you know there's nothing to be worried about or scared of, your body still reacts.

The amygdala is MUCH QUICKER than the rational, conscious decision-making part of your brain. So you feel fear before you can tell yourself there's nothing to worry about.

RELAAAAAX

BUT you can BEAT fearful feelings by taking time to relax your body. Relaxing gets rid of the tension caused by your amygdala's automatic response.

Psychologists recommend something called

PROGRESSIVE MUSCLE RELAXATION.

That's a fancy way of saying you tense your muscles, then relax them, one by one.

1 Start at your toes, and clench them downwards for a few seconds. Relax.

2 Then clench your leg muscles, and relax them.

3 Pull in your bottom muscles, stomach muscles, and continue, one by one, right up through your body to your face, and RELAX.

Breathing slowly as you do it will help calm you down more.

SPLAT

Immerse yourself in doodling and drawing, and turn these paint splatters into other things – from creatures and aliens to hats, cars and flowers.

STRETCH AND BREATHE

Give this sequence of yoya poses a try. While you're doing it, focus on BREATHING steadily and deeply, in, and then out, to unwind gently and relax. Be MINDFUL - think about your body, how it's moving, and what you can feel under your hands and feet. As you do it, let any worries drift off.

This circular sequence is called a SUN SALUTATION.

START and FINISH here.

1

2

Breathe IN, and raise your hands above your head.

Stand up tall.

11

Breathe IN. Stand up tall and raise your hands above your head.

10

9

Breathe OUT. Bring your right foot forward and stand up, keeping your chest close to your knees.

Breathe IN. This time bring your left foot forward.

68

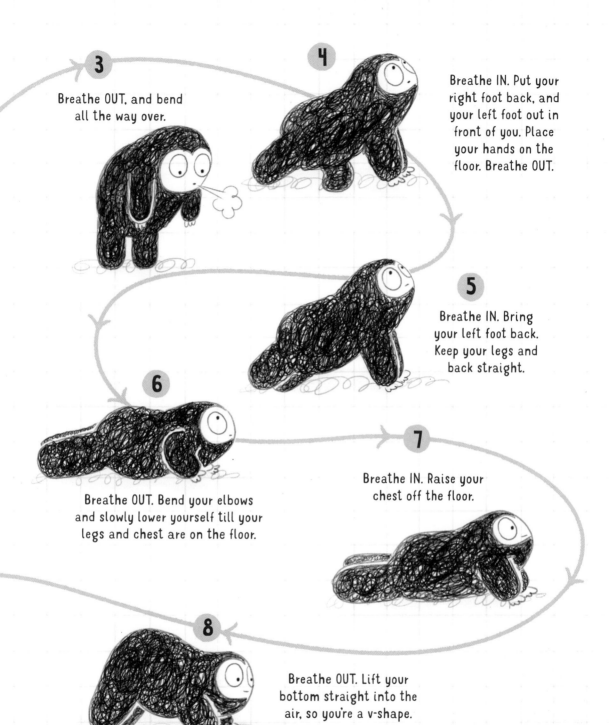

3

Breathe OUT, and bend all the way over.

4

Breathe IN. Put your right foot back, and your left foot out in front of you. Place your hands on the floor. Breathe OUT.

5

Breathe IN. Bring your left foot back. Keep your legs and back straight.

6

Breathe OUT. Bend your elbows and slowly lower yourself till your legs and chest are on the floor.

7

Breathe IN. Raise your chest off the floor.

8

Breathe OUT. Lift your bottom straight into the air, so you're a v-shape.

The more you do this the easier it'll be.

STORY MAKER

Time for some more CREATIVE distraction and brain-stretching. Use the story board here to create a story. You could draw, or write, or use a combination of both to make a cartoon strip.

Pick one of these characters to build a story around, or make up one of your own.

A mysterious spy who might be a double agent.

Someone who has been framed for a crime they didn't commit.

The sole survivor of a shipwreck.

A scientist who's discovered aliens, but hasn't told anyone else.

STORY BOARD

Putting yourself in someone else's shoes can
help you understand your own feelings more.

DOTS

Join the dots to reveal an intricate pattern. Start with dot 1, and connect them one by one in order, until they're all joined up. Concentrate on the numbers and pattern, and forget about anything else you're dwelling on.

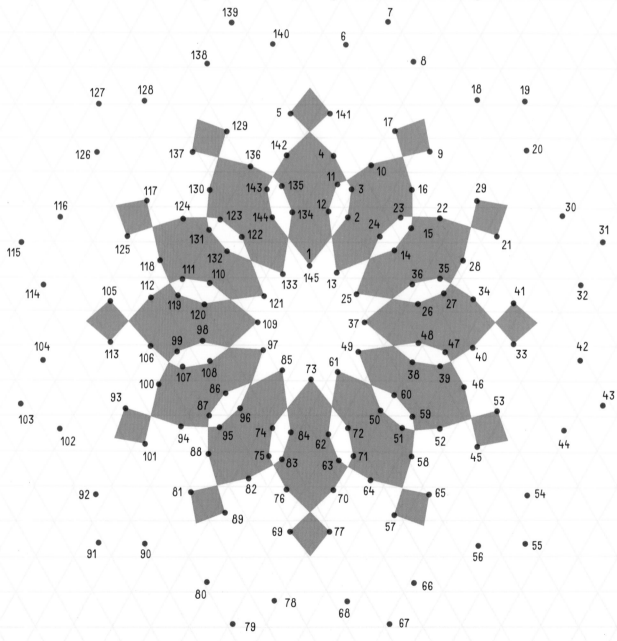

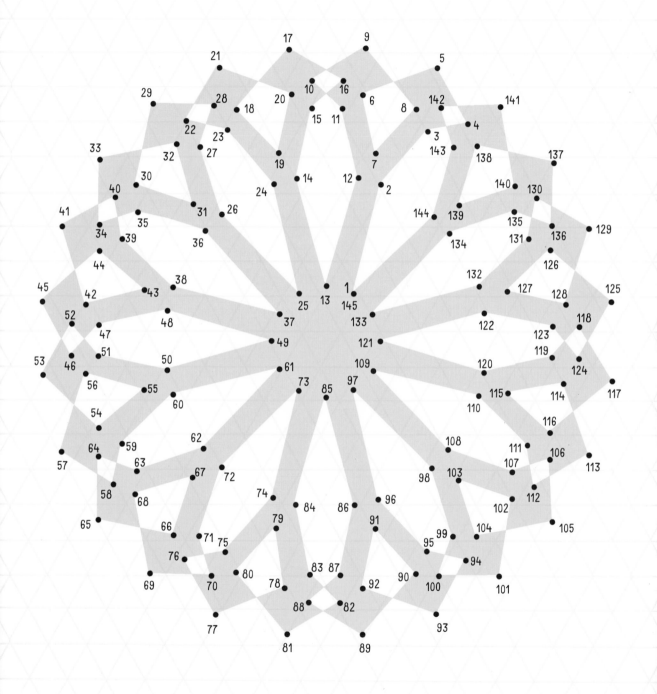

Gloopy

Cosmic

WONDERFUL WORDS

Fill this page with words you REALLY LIKE.
They could mean things that make you
smile, or just be really lovely to SAY.

Whopper

Maracas

Turnip

Thunderclap

Fork

Pickle

Gelato

Serendipity

ON YOUR MIND

Fill in the outline with anything that's in your head today.
It can be WORRIES, ideas, INVENTIONS, hopes, DREAMS,
crushes, plans - anything you're thinking about.

You could draw, scribble, doodle, or write it out in words.

Here's another one for another day.

Getting stuff OUT of your head and onto paper can help
you declutter and untangle your thoughts.

BRAIN PUZZLES

Give the puzzles on this page a try.
Keep your brain focused on these, rather than on worries.

Crack this code to work out what the message says.

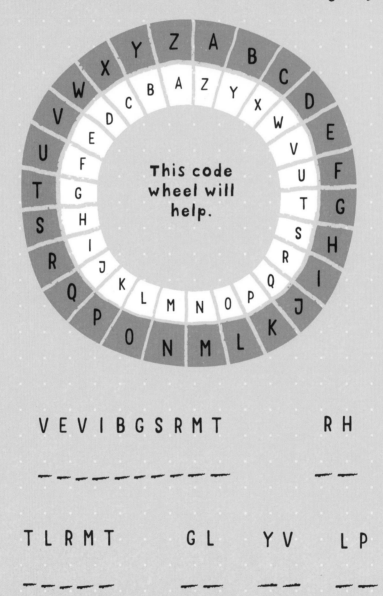

V E V I B G S R M T   R H

_ _ _ _ _ _ _ _ _ _   _ _

T L R M T   G L   Y V   L P

_ _ _ _ _   _ _   _ _   _ _

WORDSEARCH

Look for all these unworry terms:

calm

unwind

Relax

unworry

Mindful

Breathe

Laugh

Rest

The words might be across, up, down or backwards.

```
T E S B C L A M R G
S C A L M A T I R N
E E X A X U N N W O
R X U N W I N D H E
W O R R R E L F X H
X A L E R C O U N T
B R A T H F O L E A
N U C L A U G H R E
U N W O R R Y L E R
C A M M I N D O K B
```

How many words can you make using the letters of

Relaxation

Only use each letter as many times as it appears in "relaxation." What's the longest word you can make?

BREAK IT DOWN

It's often easier to write a worry down than to find the words to say it to someone out loud. Pop your worries onto these sticky notes in SHORT CHUNKS – they'll be easier to DIGEST than long, wordy, tangled thoughts.

DOODLE

Scribble freely with a pencil or pen, then doodle and draw to turn the scribble into something else, like this creature.

Use any paper in your recycling
bin for more doodling,
scribbling and scrunching.

FIDDLE STAR

When you get worried, and adrenaline builds up in your body, you often feel fidgety and nervous. But LETTING YOURSELF fidget can help you unwind, as it allows adrenaline to leave your body calmly. Follow these instructions to make an origami star, perfect for spinning, fiddling and fidgeting.

YOU WILL NEED:

A piece of paper

Scissors

A pen or pencil

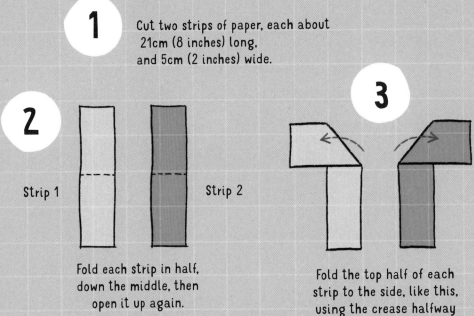

1 Cut two strips of paper, each about 21cm (8 inches) long, and 5cm (2 inches) wide.

2

Strip 1   Strip 2

Fold each strip in half, down the middle, then open it up again.

3

Fold the top half of each strip to the side, like this, using the crease halfway down as a guide.

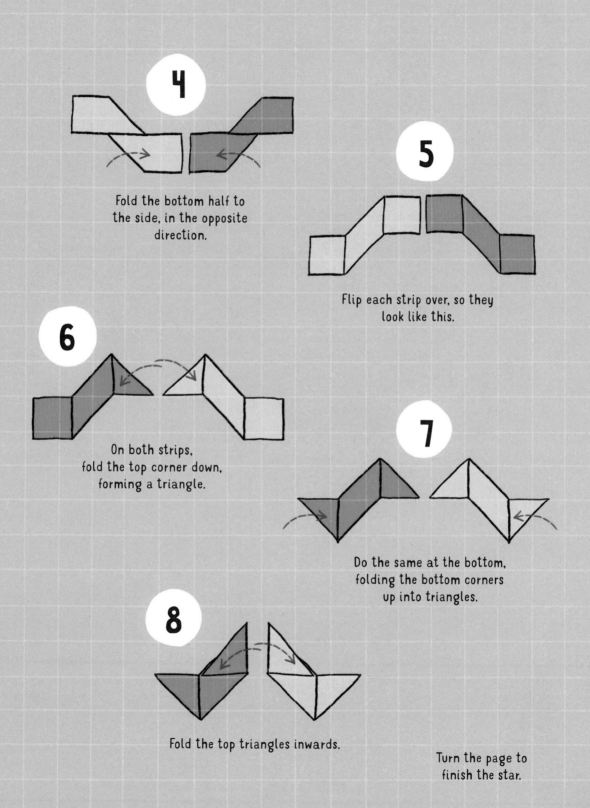

4

Fold the bottom half to the side, in the opposite direction.

5

Flip each strip over, so they look like this.

6

On both strips, fold the top corner down, forming a triangle.

7

Do the same at the bottom, folding the bottom corners up into triangles.

8

Fold the top triangles inwards.

Turn the page to finish the star.

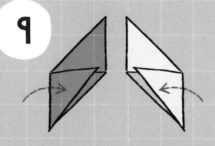

9

Fold the bottom triangles inwards too. They should overlap to form a diamond shape. Then unfold the bottom triangles again - you only need the creases.

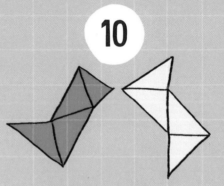

10

Flip the right hand strip over.

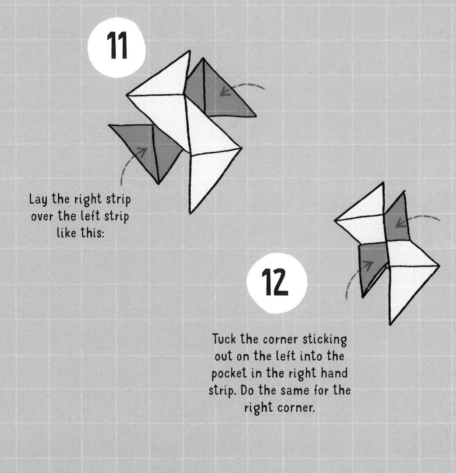

11

Lay the right strip over the left strip like this:

12

Tuck the corner sticking out on the left into the pocket in the right hand strip. Do the same for the right corner.

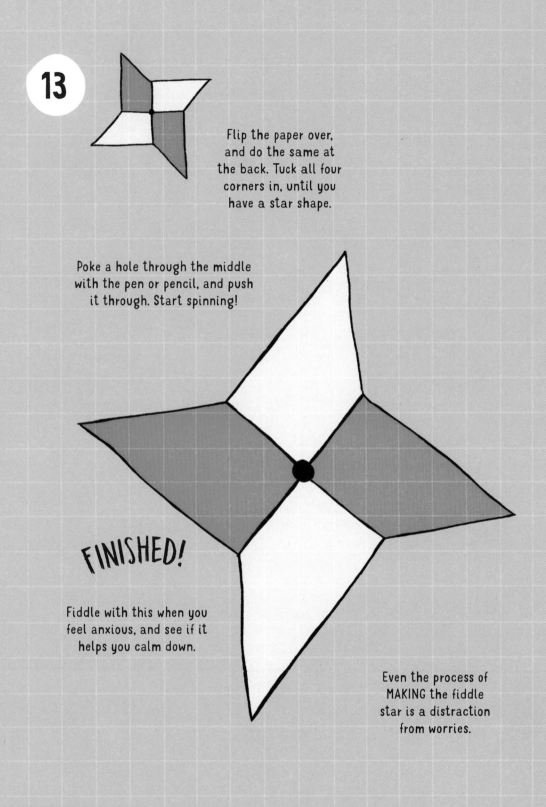

13

Flip the paper over, and do the same at the back. Tuck all four corners in, until you have a star shape.

Poke a hole through the middle with the pen or pencil, and push it through. Start spinning!

FINISHED!

Fiddle with this when you feel anxious, and see if it helps you calm down.

Even the process of MAKING the fiddle star is a distraction from worries.

THE SCIENCE OF WORRIED SLEEP

Worries often pounce when you're trying to get to sleep. They can make it hard to switch off, and sometimes give you nightmares.

Scientists still don't know exactly **HOW** or **WHY** people dream, but they think that bad dreams are your brain's way of trying to work out exactly what you are worrying about.

While you sleep, your brain digests and processes complicated thoughts and concerns, and that can turn into nightmares.

SLEEP TIPS

Sleep is really important for unworrying.
During sleep, your brain clears and sorts out
thoughts and worries that build up in the day,
making you feel better in the morning.

Here are some tips for a calm, unworried night's sleep.

AVOID SCREENS

Try not to look at a TV, phone, computer or
tablet before you get into bed.

The light of a screen **STIMULATES** your
brain, and websites, messages and social
media can feed worries you have.

GET WORRIES OUT

If particular worries pop into your head
as you try to sleep, WRITE THEM DOWN.
Then you can let them go until morning,
or forget them completely.

WIND DOWN

RELAX before you settle down. A warm bath
or shower, or drink of milk can help calm
your body down and get it ready to sleep.
You could also try smelling something
scented with calming lavender.

Turn the page
for a place
to put
nighttime
worries.

89

NIGHT WORRIES

Use the clouds to jot down any worries that come into your head while you're trying to sleep. Get them out and onto paper so you stop thinking about them, and start to SNOOOOZE instead.

WORRY SHELF

If you have a worry in your head, it can help to take it out and put it onto an imaginary shelf, where it can sit while you get on with other things. Pop your worries onto this shelf whenever you need to, and keep them shut here, at the back of this book.

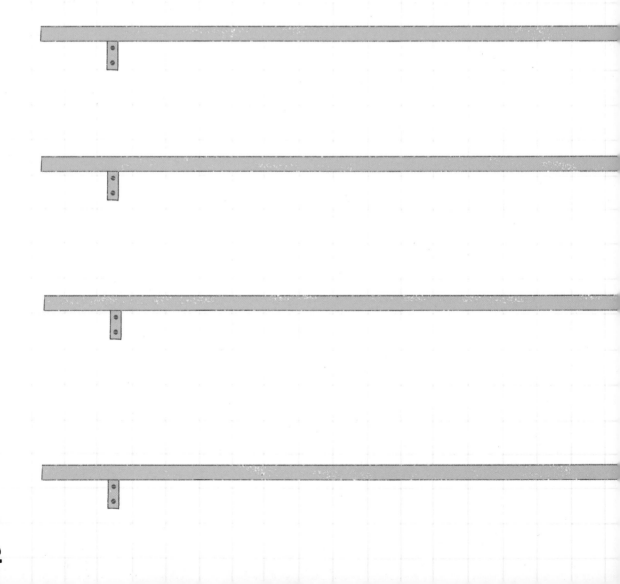

worry

You might find the worry
sorts itself out while it is
on the shelf, and when you
come back to it, it's not a
problem any more.

HELPING HAND

List five people you feel you can talk to about your worries, one on each finger. Psychologists call this your HELPING HAND – the five people who can help you feel better.

2

3

4

1

5

When you're really worried, look at this hand and find one of these people to talk to.

IF WORRIES OVERFLOW...

Most of the time worries will come and go. Taking simple steps such as breathing, relaxing, and keeping your brain focused on other things can help you feel better.

But if your worries become very overwhelming, or are making it hard for you to feel relaxed, it is really important that you TALK to someone about them. The person you talk to can comfort and support you, give you ideas to cope with your worries, or put them into perspective. Use the people on your helping hand, or any grown-up that you trust.

You could talk to your teacher at school, a counselor or a nurse, if your school has one. They will be able to give you help, advice and support, especially if worries are affecting how you concentrate or behave at school.

If worries are seriously impacting on your life, it can be a good idea to go and see your doctor. Doctors can put you in touch with specialists called psychologists and psychiatrists who can help you cope with, and get rid of, worries.

For links to websites that offer tips, advice and support to young people and parents and caregivers, go to the Usborne Quicklinks website at www.usborne.com/quicklinks.

Answers for page 78-79: The message says "Everything is going to be OK"

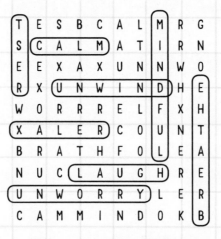

If you find 5-10 words in RELAXATION, good start.
If you find 11-20, great job. If you find more than 20, fantastic!

Additional design by Jenny Offley   Edited by Sam Taplin
American editor: Carrie Armstrong

First published in 2019 by Usborne Publishing Ltd.,
Usborne House, 83-85 Saffron Hill, London EC1N 8RT, England.

www.usborne.com Copyright © 2019 Usborne Publishing Ltd.